@Copyright 2020by Edward Carini- All rights reserved.

This document is geared towards providing exact and reliable information in regards to the topic and issue covered. The publication is sold with the idea that the publisher is not required to render accounting, officially permitted, or otherwise, qualified services. If advice is necessary, legal or professional, a practiced individual in the profession should be ordered.

Under no circumstance will any legal responsibility or blame be held against the publisher for any reparation, damages, or monetary loss due to the information herein, either directly or indirectly.

Legal Notice:

The book is copyright protected. This is only for personal use. You cannot amend, distribute, sell, use, quote or paraphrase any part or the content within this book without the consent of the author.

Disclaimer Notice:

Please note the information contained within this document is for educational and entertainment purposes only. Every attempt has been made to provide accurate, up to date and reliable complete information. No warranties of any kind are expressed or implied. Readers acknowledge that the author is not engaging in the rendering of legal, financial, medical or professional advice. The content of this book has been derived from various sources. Please consult a licensed professional before attempting any techniques outlined in this book.

CONTENTS

COOKING WITH YOUR AIR FRYER OVEN 6
    What foods can be cooked in an air fryer oven? 6
    Can you cook battered food in an air fryer oven? 6
    Can you use olive oil while air frying? 6
    How do I limit the amount of smoke when using the Air Fry Tray? 7

8 BEST Breville Smart Air Fryer Oven Recipes 9
    Breville Smart Air Fryer Chicken Wings 9
    Breville Smart Air Fryer Chicken Tenders 10
    Breville Smart Air Fryer Oven Bacon Recipe 11
    Breville Smart Air Fryer Oven Steak 11
    Breville Smart Air Fryer French Fries 12
    Breville Smart Air Fryer Fried Chicken 13
    Breville Smart Air Fryer Grilled Cheese 14
    Breville Smart Air Fryer Hamburgers 15

Breakfast recipes 16
    Tortilla de patatas with spinach 16
    Balsamic chicken with spinach & kale 17
    Sweet berry pastry 18
    Easy parsnip hash browns 18
    Peanut butter & honey porridge 19
    Egg english muffin with bacon 20
    Parsley sausage patties 21
    Quick mac & cheese 22
    Basil prosciutto crostini with mozzarella 22
    Easy french-style apple cake 23
    avocado with poached eggs 24
    toasted cinnamon bananas 25

Appetizers & side dishes 26
    Potato chips with creamy lemon dip 26
    Tasty bok choy crisps 27
    Cheese biscuits 27
    Cheesy chicken breasts with marinara sauce 28
    Cabbage & carrot canapes with amul cheese 29
    Garlic brussels sprouts 30
    Cheddar & prosciutto strips 31

- Asparagus wrapped in bacon ... 32
- Grilled sandwich with ham & cheese ... 33
- Cheese scones with chives ... 34
- Mango cashew nuts ... 35
- French beans with shallots & almonds ... 36
- Bread cheese sticks ... 37

Fish & seafood ... 38
- Parsley catfish fillets ... 38
- Old bay shrimp ... 39
- Buttery crab legs ... 40
- Smoked paprika tiger shrimp ... 41
- Crusty scallops ... 42
- Rosemary & garlic prawns ... 43
- Harissa shrimp ... 44
- Lobster tails with lemon-garlic sauce ... 45
- Breaded seafood ... 46
- Spinach & tuna balls with ricotta ... 47
- Dijon herb salmon ... 48

Meat recipes ... 49
- air fryer beef casserole ... 49
- charred onions & steak cube bbq ... 50
- beef ribeye steak ... 51
- air fryer roast beef ... 52
- parmesan breaded pork chops ... 53
- breaded pork chops ... 54
- roasted pork tenderloin ... 55
- air fryer beef burgers ... 56
- bacon-wrapped filet mignon ... 57
- lamb burgers ... 58
- Lamb chops ... 59
- Meatballs ... 60

Poultry recipes ... 61
- Saucy grilled chicken ... 61
- Mustard & thyme chicken ... 62
- Avocado & radish chicken bowl ... 63
- White wine chicken wings ... 64
- Garlic lemony chicken breast ... 65

Crispy parmesan escallops 66
Sweet chinese chicken wingettes 67
Chicken wings with buffalo sauce 68
Coconut chicken breasts 69
Asian-style chicken drumsticks 70
Chicken wings with chili-lime sauce 71
Chicken wings with honey & cashew cream 72
Chicken & cheese enchilada 73
Balsamic chicken with mozzarella cheese 74
Parmesan coated chicken cutlets 75

Vegetables 76
jalapeño poppers 76
air fried cauliflower rice 77
air fried thyme potatoes 78
buttered cauliflower 78
tangy brussels sprout 79
spiced zucchini 80
green beans with carrots 81
mixed veggies combo 82
Sage honey sweet potatoes 83
Greek roasted broccoli 84
Balsamic cauliflower 85

Snacks & appetizers 86
onion strudel 86
parmesan baked onion 87
garlic kale chips 88
pita chips 88
almond onion rings 89
jicama fries 90
air fried chickpeas 90
banana chips 91
Baked okra 92
Salmon croquettes 92
Crispy broccoli florets 93
Eggplant fries 94
Fish nuggets 94
Herb chicken wings 95

Desserts 97
    Apple treat with raisins 97
    Pan-fried bananas 97
    Delicious banana pastry with berries 98
    Cinnamon & honey apples with hazelnuts 98
    Maple pecan pie 99
    Easy mocha cake 99
    Apricot crumble with blackberries 100
    Handmade donuts 101
    Mouthwatering chocolate soufflé 101
    Choco lava cakes 102

COOKING WITH YOUR AIR FRYER OVEN

WHAT FOODS CAN BE COOKED IN AN AIR FRYER OVEN?

You can use the air fry setting on your oven for most foods that can traditionally be deep-fried. Some of our favorite recipes include:
- Chicken wings, chicken nuggets or pizza bites
- French fries, onion rings or sweet potato fries
- Brussel sprouts, kale, or zucchini fries

CAN YOU COOK BATTERED FOOD IN AN AIR FRYER OVEN?

Crispy food needs enough oil to bind batters and coatings, but not too much or you'll end up with soggy results. If the food has a crumbly or floury outside texture, try spraying it with a little bit more oil.

If you're making air fried food from scratch, spray your homemade items with a light coating of oil (too much and the food won't get crispy) and arrange foods so the hot air circulates around each piece as much as possible.

CAN YOU USE OLIVE OIL WHILE AIR FRYING?

Using cooking oils that can stand up to high temperatures is key while air frying, so avocado, grapeseed, and peanut oil are great for achieving crispy goodness. For best results, brush on lightly or spray an even coat of cooking spray made from these oils. Extra virgin olive oil is not an air fry-friendly oil due to its low smoke point, but *extra light* olive oil can be used for air frying because of its high smoke point. Other types of olive oil and some vegetable oils smoke at lower temperatures, meaning they will cause food to dry up quickly and prevent them from getting crispy.

CAN YOU USE ALUMINUM FOIL IN AN AIR FRYER OVEN?

Air fry works best on dark pans because they get and stay hot very quickly. Shiny foil reflects heat off the bakeware, which may change your results. When cooking with the Air fry Tray, we suggest putting a baking sheet on a rack a couple of positions below your tray. You can line that sheet with foil or parchment (or both) to catch any drips or crumbs, but you should never put aluminum foil, liners, or bakeware on the oven bottom. Items in this location can cause issues with air circulation and direct heat in any oven. Always keep the bottom of the oven clear so the air can circulate properly.

How do I keep my air frying oven clean?
Before using the air fry feature, place a cookie or baking sheet a rack or two under the Air Fry Tray to catch crumbs or drips. This will keep the bottom of the oven clean and free of fallen bits that can burn or cause odors later. Remember, do not place pans directly on the oven bottom to keep heat circulating correctly.

How do I clean the Air Fry Tray?
The Air Fry Tray is dishwasher safe, but for optimal cleaning, we recommend washing it by hand. It's designed to hold foods that already have some oil on them, which should keep food from sticking.

HOW dO I LIMIT THE AMOUNT OF SMOKE WHEN USING THE AIR FRY TRAY?

Air fry uses really hot air to cook food fast and make it crunchy. Although air fry uses hot air to cook, remember that you are still frying your food so that it gets crispy! When some high-fat or greasy foods (like fresh wings) meet that hot air inside an oven, some smoke is normal. If air fry is making a lot of smoke, try these tips:
- When using the Air Fry Tray, put a baking sheet on a rack or two below the Air Fry Tray. This keeps drips and crumbs from landing on the oven bottom, where they can burn and create smoke. For additional protection, place some foil-lined parchment paper on the baking sheet. Parchment paper traps oil and keeps it from smoking.
- Use cooking oils that can stand up to high temperatures like avocado, grapeseed, and peanut oils. Cooking sprays made from these oils are available at the grocery store.
- Keep foil, parchment paper, and bakeware off the bottom of the oven. The oven bottom needs to stay clear so air can circulate.

- Don't overcrowd the food on your baking sheet or on the Air Fry Tray. If air can't circulate around each item, the cooking and crisping process may slow down and allow more grease to settle or drip.
- If your catch-tray is smoking, try placing parchment paper on it to hold grease. For extra-moist foods, you may have to use more. It's worth it!
- Some foods, like fresh wings and some vegetables, have a lot of moisture and may drip more than you expect. For items that might drip, use a pan with low sides if you're not using an Air Fry Tray.
- Air fry uses super-heated air, so if your oven bottom already has drips or crumbs on it (it happens!), those can smoke. Keep your oven bottom clean.
- If you have an oven vent, use it when cooking with air fry, like you would when using the cooktop.

8 BEST BREVILLE SMART AIR FRYER OVEN RECIPES

BREVILLE SMART AIR FRYER CHICKEN WINGS

Ingredients:

- 3 lbs chicken wing pieces cut into drumettes & flats
- Olive oil cooking spray
- 2 tbsp melted butter
- 1 tbsp seasoned salt
- ½ cup flour
- 3 tbsp maple syrup
- 3 tbsp hot sauce

Directions:

1. Remove tips from chicken wings and separate flats and drumettes. Spray olive oil to lightly coat the inside of your air fry basket. Place wings in a medium-size bowl and spray them lightly with olive oil spray.
2. After that, mix the salt and the flour in a medium-size bowl and toss the wings in the flour mixture to be lightly coated. Place your wings in the fryer basket and then into the Breville Smart Air Fryer oven. Press the M button and adjust the cooking time to 25 minutes at 325 degrees Fahrenheit.
3. Keep pausing and flipping the wings after every 5-6 minutes for even cooking. Turn the temperature to 400 degrees once the wings have become slightly brown. While the wings are cooking, mix the melted butter, maple syrup, and hot sauce.
4. Take the wings out of the oven when they are crispy and cooked through. Toss the fully cooked wings with the sauce. Finally, serve your chicken wings with blue cheese dressing if needed.

BREVILLE SMART AIR FRYER CHICKEN TENdERS

Ingredients:

- 6 chicken tenders, raw
- 3 large eggs
- ½ cup flour, white
- 1 cup panko breadcrumbs
- 1 tsp sea salt
- ½ tsp black pepper
- 1 tsp olive oil
- ½ cup milk

Directions:

1. In a medium-size bowl, combine panko breadcrumbs with olive oil and mix the eggs with milk in a separate bowl. Pour flour into a pot or pan and dip chicken tenders into the flour first, then into the egg mixture, and finally into the panko breadcrumbs mixture. Preheat your air fryer by setting it to 400 degrees Fahrenheit for about 5 minutes.
2. Put the breaded tenders into the fry basket and place the fry basket into the Breville Smart Air Fryer XL. Press the M button and scroll to the French fries icon. Press the power button to start and adjust the cooking time to 14 minutes at 400 degrees Fahrenheit.
3. Flip the tenders over after 7 minutes of cooking to brown the other side. Remove the tenders when the juices run clear and the pink flesh has disappeared. You can now serve your fully cooked tenders with your favorite sauce.

BREVILLE SMART AIR FRYER OVEN BACON RECIPE

Ingredients:

- Bacon (as much as you desire)

Directions:

1. Preheat your air fryer to 200 degrees Celsius or 390 degrees Fahrenheit. Place bacon on a single layer inside the air fryer basket (no problem if some of them fold or overlap). Adjust the air fryer to 350 degrees Fahrenheit and cook for about 10 minutes.
2. Halfway through cooking, flip the bacon and continue cooking for an additional 7 minutes until the bacon turns crisp. Transfer your fully cooked bacon into a plate that is lined with paper towels to drain the excess grease. Serve your bacon while still hot.

BREVILLE SMART AIR FRYER OVEN STEAK

Ingredients:

- Ribeye steak or New York strip steak
- Kosher salt to taste
- Butter
- Paprika
- Black pepper to taste
- Garlic powder to taste

Directions:

1. Bring the steak to room temperature so that it can cook evenly. Spray olive oil on all sides of the steak and season with black pepper, kosher salt, paprika, and garlic powder. Preheat your air fryer to 400 degrees Fahrenheit for 3 minutes.
2. Put the steak inside the air fryer basket and cook for 12 minutes. Flip the steak halfway through cooking to ensure all sides are evenly cooked. Top your steak with butter and serve immediately.

BREVILLE SMART AIR FRYER FRENCH FRIES

Ingredients:

- 2-3 Yukon gold potatoes, scrubbed
- 1 tbsp extra-virgin olive oil
- Salt & pepper to taste
- Paprika, garlic powder and other seasonings you may like

Directions:

1. Preheat your air fryer by setting it to 360 degrees Fahrenheit. Chop the potatoes to form French fry shapes of approximately 0.5 inches thick. Place the raw potato slices in a bowl containing warm water for 10 minutes.
2. Drain the potato slices and transfer them into a large bowl. Drizzle the raw potato slices in a bowl with olive oil and season generously with salt, pepper and your favorite seasonings like chili powder, paprika, or garlic powder. Toss properly to coat the potato slices.
3. Have your seasoned potato slices arranged in a single layer on the air fryer basket. Cook them for 15 minutes maintaining the temperature of 360 degrees Fahrenheit. As soon as the timer has elapsed, remove the crisp fries from the air fryer using a spatula and serve immediately alongside your favorite dipping sauce.

BREVILLE SMART AIR FRYER FRIEd CHICKEN

Ingredients:

- 4 pieces of chicken legs, thighs, or breasts
- 1 piece egg
- 1 cup all-purpose flour
- 1 tsp seasoning salt
- 2 tbsp old bay Cajun seasoning
- Peanut, coconut, or canola oil in mister or spray bottle

Directions:

1. Preheat the air fryer to 380 degrees Fahrenheit. Pat each piece of chicken dry with a paper towel and set the pieces on a shallow tray. In a large bowl, mix 2 tsp old bay seasoning, 1 tsp seasoning salt, and 1 cup all-purpose flour. Make sure to thoroughly whisk the ingredients together.
2. Beat the egg in a separate bowl. Then, dredge the chicken pieces in three steps: first, drop the pieces into the flour mixture and put them back into the tray: next, dredge the chicken pieces in the egg; and finally, drop the pieces back into the flour and shake off the excess flour.
3. Spray the chicken pieces with the oil, ensuring each piece gets covered completely. Put the chicken pieces into the bottom of the fryer basket and set the air fryer to 180 degrees Fahrenheit and cook for 25 minutes. An instant meat thermometer can help you know whether it has reached 180 degrees Fahrenheit.
4. Remove the fried chicken from the air fryer. Be careful while taking out the fried chicken from the air fryer because it can be hot. Serve immediately while still hot and enjoy.

BREVILLE SMART AIR FRYER GRILLEd CHEESE

Ingredients:

- 2 bread slices
- 50 g butter or margarine
- 100 g cheese
- 2 slices tomato
- 1 slice ham

Directions:

1. Preheat your air fryer to 360 degrees Fahrenheit or 180 degrees Celsius, which could take about 3 minutes depending on the air fryer model you are using. Apply butter on one side of each bread slice. Make sure you use enough butter to get them covered completely.
2. Slice the cheese and put it between the two bread slices. Ensure the buttered sides are facing the outside of the sandwich. Put the sandwich in the air fryer basket and cook for 8 minutes.
3. Within the first 4 minutes of cooking, open the basket and flip the grilled cheese over. Finally, cook for the remaining 4 minutes. Remove the grilled cheese when cooked and let it cool before you can enjoy.

BREVILLE SMART AIR FRYER HAMBURGERS

Ingredients:

- Ground beef
- Salt
- Pepper
- Cheese
- Buns

Directions:

1. Preheat your air fryer to 180 degrees Celsius or 350 degrees Fahrenheit. Combine the beef, black pepper and salt in a bowl and arrange the beef mixture to form four burger patties. Spray the basket of the air fryer with a little oil to lightly coat.
2. Add the burgers into the air fryer basket. Let it cook for 8-12 minutes depending on your preferred level of doneness. Flip them over halfway through cooking to ensure they are evenly cooked.
3. One minute before they are fully cooked, take out the air fryer basket and top each burger with cheese. Put the air fryer basket back and cook until done. Finally, build your burgers & serve to enjoy.

BREAKFAST RECIPES

TORTILLA dE PATATAS WITH SPINACH

Cooking Time: 25 minutes   Serves: 4

Ingredients:
- 3 cups potato cubes, boiled
- 2 cups spinach, chopped
- 5 eggs, lightly beaten
- ¼ cup heavy cream
- 1 cup mozzarella cheese, grated
- ½ cup fresh parsley, chopped
- Salt and black pepper to taste

Directions:
1. Preheat breville on bake function to 390 f. Place the potatoes in a greased baking dish. In a bowl, whisk eggs, heavy cream, spinach, mozzarella cheese, parsley, salt, and pepper and pour over the potatoes. Press start. Cook for 16 minutes until nice and golden. Serve warm.

BALSAMIC CHICKEN WITH SPINACH & KALE

Cooking Time: 20 minutesServes: 1

Ingredients:
- ½ cup baby spinach
- ½ cup romaine lettuce, shredded
- 3 large kale leaves, chopped
- 1 chicken breast, cut into cubes
- 2 tbsp olive oil
- 1 tsp balsamic vinegar
- 1 garlic clove, minced
- Salt and black pepper to taste

Directions:
1. Place the chicken, some olive oil, garlic, salt, and pepper in a bowl; toss to combine. Put on a lined baking dish and cook in the breville for 14 minutes at 390f on bake function.
2. Meanwhile, place the greens in a large bowl. Add the remaining olive oil and balsamic vinegar. Season with salt and pepper and toss to combine. Top with the sliced chicken and serve.

SWEET BERRY PASTRY

Cooking Time: 20 minutes

Serves: 3

Ingredients:
- 3 pastry dough sheets
- 2 tbsp strawberries, mashed
- 2 tbsp raspberries, mashed
- ¼ tsp vanilla extract
- 2 cups cream cheese, softened
- 1 tbsp honey

Directions:
1. Preheat breville oven on bake function to 375 f. Spread the cream cheese on the dough sheets. In a bowl, combine berries, honey, and vanilla. Divide the mixture between the pastry sheets. Pinch the ends of the sheets to form puff. Place in the breville oven and cook for 15 minutes.

EASY PARSNIP HASH BROWNS

Cooking Time: 20 minutes

Serves: 2

Ingredients:
- 1 large parsnip, grated
- 3 eggs, beaten
- ½ tsp garlic powder
- ¼ tsp nutmeg
- 1 tbsp olive oil
- 1 cup flour
- Salt and black pepper to taste

Directions:
1. In a bowl, combine flour, eggs, parsnip, nutmeg, and garlic powder. Season with salt and pepper. Form patties out of the mixture. Drizzle the basket with olive oil and arrange the patties inside. Press start. Cook for 15 minutes on airfry function at 360 f. Serve with garlic mayo.

PEANUT BUTTER & HONEY PORRIdGE

Cooking Time: 5 minutes

Serves: 4

Ingredients:
- 2 cups steel-cut oats
- 1 cup flax seeds
- 1 tbsp peanut butter
- 1 tbsp butter
- 4 cups milk
- 4 tbsp honey

Directions:
1. Preheat breville on bake function to 390 f. Combine all of the ingredients in an ovenproof bowl. Place in the breville oven and press start. Cook for 7 minutes. Stir and serve.

EGG ENGLISH MUFFIN WITH BACON

Cooking Time: 10 minutes

Serves: 1

Ingredients:
- 1 egg
- 1 english muffin
- 2 slices of bacon
- Salt and black pepper to taste

Directions:
1. Preheat breville on bake function to 395 f. Crack the egg into a ramekin. Place the muffin, egg and bacon in the oven. Cook for 9 minutes. Let cool slightly so you can assemble the sandwich.
2. Cut the muffin in half. Place the egg on one half and season with salt and pepper. Arrange the bacon on top. Top with the other muffin half.

PARSLEY SAUSAGE PATTIES

Cooking Time: 20 minutes

Serves: 4

Ingredients:
- 1 lb ground italian sausage
- ¼ cup breadcrumbs
- 1 tsp dried parsley
- 1 tsp red pepper flakes
- Salt and black pepper to taste
- ¼ tsp garlic powder
- 1 egg, beaten

Directions:
1. Preheat breville on bake function to 350 f. Line a baking sheet with parchment paper. Combine all the ingredients in a large bowl.
2. Make patties out of the sausage mixture and arrange them on the baking sheet. Press start. Cook for 15 minutes until golden.

QUICK MAC & CHEESE

Cooking Time: 15 minutes

Serves: 2

Ingredients:
- 1 cup macaroni, cooked
- 1 cup cheddar cheese, grated
- ½ cup warm milk
- 1 tbsp parmesan cheese, grated
- Salt and black pepper to taste

Directions:
1. Preheat breville on airfry function to 350 f. Add the macaroni to an ovenproof baking dish. Stir in the cheddar cheese and milk. Season with salt and pepper. Place the dish in the breville oven and press start. Cook for 10 minutes. Sprinkle with parmesan cheese and serve.

BASIL PROSCIUTTO CROSTINI WITH MOZZARELLA

Cooking Time: 7 minutes

Serves: 1

Ingredients:
- ½ cup tomatoes, chopped
- 3 oz mozzarella cheese, chopped
- 3 prosciutto slices, chopped
- 1 tbsp olive oil
- 1 tsp dried basil
- 6 small slices of french bread

Directions:
1. Preheat breville on toast function to 350 f. Place in the bread slices and toast them for 5 minutes. Top the bread with tomatoes, prosciutto, and mozzarella. Sprinkle with basil. Drizzle with olive oil. Return to oven and cook for 1 more minute, enough to become melty and warm.

EASY FRENCH-STYLE APPLE CAKE

Cooking Time: 25 minutes

Serves: 6

Ingredients:
- 2 ¾ oz flour
- 5 tbsp sugar
- 1 ¼ oz butter
- 3 tbsp cinnamon
- 2 whole apple, sliced

Directions:
1. Preheat breville on bake function to 360 f. In a bowl, mix 3 tbsp sugar, butter, and flour; form pastry using the batter. Roll out the pastry on a floured surface and transfer it to the basket.
2. Arrange the apple slices atop. Cover apples with sugar and cinnamon and press start. Cook cook for 20 minutes. Sprinkle with powdered sugar and mint and serve.

AVOCAdO WITH POACHEd EGGS

Cooking Time: 10 minutes

Serves: 1

Ingredients:
- 2 eggs
- 1/2 avocado
- 2 slices bread
- 1 bunch spinach
- Pinch of salt
- Pinch of pepper

Directions:
1. Preheat the air fryer oven to 350°f.
2. Bring a pan of water to a boil.
3. Place bread on a pan and toast it in the oven for 10 minutes. Once the water is boiling, whisk it around in a circle.
4. Drop one egg in the hole and turn the heat to low, and then poach for 2 minutes.
5. Repeat with the second egg.
6. Mash avocado and spread it over the toast while the eggs poach.
7. Add the eggs to the toast and top with spinach.

TOASTEd CINNAMON BANANAS

Cooking Time: 10 minutes

Serves: 1

Ingredients:
- 1 ripe banana
- 1 tsp. Lemon juice
- 2 tsp. Honey
- 1 tbsp. Ground cinnamon

Directions:
1. Preheat the air fryer oven to 350°f.
2. Slice bananas lengthwise, then put them on a greased baking sheet.
3. Brush each slice with lemon juice.
4. Drizzle honey and sprinkle cinnamon over each slice.
5. Bake for 10 minutes.

APPETIZERS & SIdE dISHES

POTATO CHIPS WITH CREAMY LEMON dIP

Cooking Time: 25 minutes

Serves: 3

Ingredients:
- 3 large potatoes
- 1 cup sour cream
- 2 scallions, white part minced
- 3 tbsp olive oil.
- ½ tsp lemon juice
- Salt and black pepper

Directions:
1. Preheat breville on airfry function to 350 f. Cut the potatoes into thin slices; do not peel them. Brush them with olive oil and season with salt and pepper. Arrange on the frying basket.
2. Press start on the oven and cook for 20-25 minutes. Season with salt and pepper. To prepare the dip, mix together the sour cream, olive oil, scallions, lemon juice, salt, and pepper.

TASTY BOK CHOY CRISPS

Cooking Time: 10 minutes Serves: 2

Ingredients:
- 2 tbsp olive oil
- 4 cups packed bok choy
- 1 tsp italian seasoning
- 1 tbsp yeast flakes
- Sea salt to taste

Directions:
1. In a bowl, mix olive oil, bok choy, yeast, and italian seasoning. Dump the coated kale in frying basket. Set the temperature of breville toaster oven to 360 f on airfry function and press start. Cook for 5-8 minutes until crispy. Serve sprinkled with sea salt.

CHEESE BISCUITS

Cooking Time: 35 minutes

Serves: 6

Ingredients:
- ½ cup + 1 tbsp butter
- 2 tbsp sugar
- 3 cups flour
- 1 ⅓ cups buttermilk
- ½ cup cheddar cheese, grated

Directions:
1. Preheat breville on airfry function to 380 f. Lay a parchment paper on a baking plate. In a bowl, mix sugar, flour, ½ cup butter, cheese, and buttermilk to form a batter. Make balls from the batter and roll in the flour. Place the balls in the baking plate and flatten into biscuit shapes. Sprinkle with cheese and the remaining butter. Place in the oven and press start. Cook for 30 minutes, tossing every 10 minutes. Serve chilled.

CHEESY CHICKEN BREASTS WITH MARINARA SAUCE

Cooking Time: 25 minutes

Serves: 2

Ingredients:
- 2 chicken breasts, beaten into ½ inch thick
- 1 egg, beaten
- ½ cup breadcrumbs
- Salt and black pepper to taste
- 2 tbsp marinara sauce
- 2 tbsp grana padano cheese, grated
- 2 mozzarella cheese slices

Directions:
1. Dip the breasts into the egg, then into the crumbs and arrange on the fryer basket. Select airfry function, adjust the temperature to 400 f, and press start. Cook for 5 minutes, turn over, and drizzle with marinara sauce, grana padano and mozzarella cheeses. Cook for 5 more minutes.

CABBAGE & CARROT CANAPES WITH AMUL CHEESE

Cooking Time: 15 minutes

Serves: 2

Ingredients:
- 1 whole cabbage, cut in rounds
- 1 cube amul cheese
- ½ carrot, cubed
- ¼ onion, cubed
- ¼ bell pepper, cubed
- 1 tbsp fresh basil, chopped

Directions:
1. Preheat breville on airfry function to 360 f. In a bowl, mix onion, carrot, bell pepper, and cheese. Toss to coat everything evenly. Add cabbage to the frying basket. Top with the veggie mixture and place in the oven. Press start and cook for 8 minutes. Serve topped with basil.

GARLIC BRUSSELS SPROUTS

Cooking Time: 25 minutes

Serves: 4

Ingredients:
- 1 pound brussels sprouts
- 1 garlic clove, minced
- 2 tbsp olive oil
- Salt and black pepper to taste

Directions:
1. Wash the brussels sprouts thoroughly under cold water and trim off the outer leaves, keeping only the head of the sprouts. In a bowl, mix olive oil and garlic. Season with salt and pepper.
2. Add in the prepared sprouts let rest for 5 minutes. Place the coated sprouts in the frying basket. Select airfry function, adjust the temperature to 380 f, and press start. Cook for 15 minutes.

CHEddAR & PROSCIUTTO STRIPS

Cooking Time: 50 minutes

Serves: 6

Ingredients:
- 1 lb cheddar cheese
- 12 prosciutto slices
- 1 cup flour
- 2 eggs, beaten
- 4 tbsp olive oil
- 1 cup breadcrumbs

Directions:
1. Cut the cheese into 6 equal pieces. Wrap each piece with 2 prosciutto slices. Place them in the freezer just enough to set, about 5 minutes; note that they mustn't be frozen.
2. Preheat breville on airfry function to 390 f. Dip the strips into flour first, then in eggs, and coat with breadcrumbs. Place in the frying basket and drizzle with olive oil. Press start and cook for 10 minutes or until golden brown. Serve with tomato dip.

ASPARAGUS WRAPPEd IN BACON

Cooking Time: 25 minutes

Serves: 4

Ingredients:
- 20 spears asparagus
- 4 bacon slices
- 1 tbsp olive oil
- 1 tbsp sesame oil
- 1 garlic clove, minced

Directions:
1. Preheat breville on airfry function to 380 f. In a bowl, mix the oils, sugar, and garlic. Separate the asparagus into 4 bunches (5 spears in 1 bunch) and wrap each bunch with a bacon slice.
2. Drizzle the bunches with oil mix. Put them in the frying basket and place in the oven. Press start and cook for 8 minutes. Serve warm.

GRILLEd SANdWICH WITH HAM & CHEESE

Cooking Time: 15 minutes

Serves: 2

Ingredients:
- 4 bread slices
- ¼ cup butter
- 2 ham slices
- 2 mozzarella cheese slices

Directions:
1. Preheat breville on airfry function to 360 degrees f. Place 2 bread slices on a flat surface. Spread butter on the exposed surfaces. Lay cheese and ham on two of the slices.
2. Cover with the other 2 slices to form sandwiches. Place the sandwiches in the frying basket. Select bake function, adjust the temperature to 380 f, and press start. Cook for 5 minutes.

CHEESE SCONES WITH CHIVES

Cooking Time: 25 minutes

Serves: 6

Ingredients:
- 1 cup flour
- Salt and black pepper to taste
- 3 tbsp butter
- 1 tsp fresh chives, chopped
- 1 whole egg
- 1 tbsp milk
- 1 cup cheddar cheese, shredded

Directions:
1. Preheat breville on airfry function to 340 f. In a bowl, mix butter, flour, cheddar cheese, chives, milk, and egg to get a sticky dough. Dust a flat surface with flour. Roll the dough into small balls. Place the balls in the frying basket and place in the oven. Press start and cook for 20 minutes.

MANGO CASHEW NUTS

Cooking Time: 25 minutes

Serves: 2

Ingredients:
- 1 cup greek yogurt
- 2 tbsp mango powder
- ½ cup cashew nuts
- Salt and black pepper to taste
- 1 tsp coriander powder
- ½ tsp masala powder

Directions:
1. Preheat breville on bake function to 360 f. In a bowl, mix all powders. Season with salt and pepper. Add cashews and toss to coat. Place in the oven and press start. Cook for 15 minutes.

FRENCH BEANS WITH SHALLOTS & ALMONdS

Cooking Time: 25 minutes

Serves: 4

Ingredients:
- 1 ½ pounds french beans
- 2 shallots, chopped
- 2 tbsp olive oil
- ½ cup almonds, toasted

Directions:
1. Preheat breville on airfry function to 400 f. Blanch the beans in boiling water for 5-6 minutes. Drain and mix with oil and shallots in a baking sheet. Cook for 10 minutes. Serve with almonds.

BREAd CHEESE STICKS

Cooking Time: 5 minutes

Serves: 6

Ingredients:
- 6 (6 oz) bread cheese
- 2 tbsp butter, melted
- 2 cups panko crumbs

Directions:
1. With a knife, cut the cheese into equal-sized sticks. Brush each stick with butter and dip into the panko crumbs. Arrange the sticks in a single layer on the basket tray. Select airfry function, adjust the temperature to 390 f, and press start. Cook for 10-12 minutes. Serve warm.

FISH & SEAFOOd

PARSLEY CATFISH FILLETS

Cooking Time: 25 minutes   Serves: 4

Ingredients:
- 4 catfish fillets, rinsed and dried
- ¼ cup seasoned fish fry
- 1 tbsp olive oil
- 1 tbsp fresh parsley, chopped

Directions:
1. Add seasoned fish fry and fillets in a large ziploc bag; massage well to coat. Place the fillets in the breville basket and cook for 14-16 minutes at 360 f on airfry function. Top with parsley.

OLd BAY SHRIMP

Cooking Time: 10 minutes

Serves: 4

Ingredients:
- 1 lb jumbo shrimp
- Salt to taste
- ¼ tsp old bay seasoning
- ⅓ tsp smoked paprika
- ¼ tsp chili powder
- 1 tbsp olive oil

Directions:
1. Preheat breville on airfry function to 390 f. In a bowl, add the shrimp, paprika, oil, salt, old bay seasoning, and chili powder; mix well. Place the shrimp in the oven and cook for 5 minutes.

BUTTERY CRAB LEGS

Cooking Time: 15 minutes

Serves: 4

Ingredients:
- 3 pounds crab legs
- 1 cup butter, melted

Directions:
1. Preheat breville on airfry function to 380 f. Dip the crab legs in salted water and let stay for a few minutes. Drain, pat dry, and place the legs in the basket and press start. Cook for 10 minutes. Pour the butter over crab legs and serve.

SMOKEd PAPRIKA TIGER SHRIMP

Cooking Time: 10 minutes

Serves: 4

Ingredients:
- 1 lb tiger shrimp
- 2 tbsp olive oil
- ¼ tbsp garlic powder
- 1 tbsp smoked paprika
- 2 tbsp fresh parsley, chopped
- Sea salt to taste

Directions:
1. Preheat breville on airfry function to 380 f. Mix garlic powder, smoked paprika, salt, parsley, and olive oil in a large bowl. Add in the shrimp and toss to coat. Place the shrimp in the frying basket press start. Fry for 6-7 minutes. Serve with salad.

CRUSTY SCALLOPS

Cooking Time: 20 minutes

Serves: 4

Ingredients:
- 12 fresh scallops
- 3 tbsp flour
- Salt and black pepper to taste
- 1 egg, lightly beaten
- 1 cup breadcrumbs

Directions:
1. Coat the scallops with flour. Dip into the egg, then into the breadcrumbs. Arrange them on the frying basket and spray with cooking spray. Cook for 12 minutes at 360 f on airfry function.

ROSEMARY & GARLIC PRAWNS

Cooking Time: 15 minutes + chilling time

Serves: 2

Ingredients:
- 8 large prawns
- 2 garlic cloves, minced
- 1 rosemary sprig, chopped
- 1 tbsp butter, melted
- Salt and black pepper to taste

Directions:
1. Combine garlic, butter, rosemary, salt, and pepper in a bowl. Add in the prawns and mix to coat. Cover the bowl and refrigerate for 1 hour. Preheat breville on airfry function to 350 f. Remove the prawns from the fridge and transfer to the frying basket. Cook for 6-8 minutes.

HARISSA SHRIMP

Cooking Time: 15 minutes

Serves: 4

Ingredients:
- 1 ¼ lb tiger shrimp
- ¼ tsp harissa powder
- ½ tsp old bay seasoning
- Salt to taste
- 1 tbsp olive oil

Directions:
1. Preheat your breville oven to 390 f on airfry function. In a bowl, mix the ingredients. Place the mixture in the cooking basket and cook for 5 minutes. Serve with a drizzle of lemon juice.

LOBSTER TAILS WITH LEMON-GARLIC SAUCE

Cooking Time: 15 minutes

Serves: 4

Ingredients:
- 1 lb lobster tails
- 1 garlic clove, minced
- 1 tbsp butter
- Salt and black pepper to taste
- ½ tbsp lemon juice

Directions:
1. Add all the ingredients to a food processor, except for lobster and blend well. Wash lobster and halve using meat knife; clean the skin of the lobster and cover with the marinade.
2. Preheat your breville to 380 f. Place the lobster in the cooking basket and press start. Cook for 10 minutes on airfry function. Serve with fresh herbs.

BREAdEd SEAFOOd

Cooking Time: 15 minutes

Serves: 4

Ingredients:
- 1 lb scallops, mussels, fish fillets, prawns, shrimp
- 2 eggs, lightly beaten
- Salt and black pepper to taste
- 1 cup breadcrumbs mixed with zest of 1 lemon

Directions:
1. Dip the seafood pieces into the eggs and season with salt and black pepper. Coat in the crumbs and spray with cooking spray. Arrange them on the frying basket and press start. Cook for 10 minutes at 400 f on airfry function. Serve with lemon wedges.

SPINACH & TUNA BALLS WITH RICOTTA

Cooking Time: 20 minutes

Serves: 4

Ingredients:
- 14 oz store-bought crescent dough
- ½ cup spinach, steamed
- 1 cup ricotta cheese, crumbled
- ¼ tsp garlic powder
- 1 tsp fresh oregano, chopped
- ½ cup canned tuna, drained

Directions:
1. Preheat breville on airfry function to 350 f. Roll the dough onto a lightly floured flat surface. Combine the ricotta cheese, spinach, tuna, oregano, salt, and garlic powder together in a bowl.
2. Cut the dough into 4 equal pieces. Divide the mixture between the dough pieces. Make sure to place the filling in the center. Fold the dough and secure with a fork. Place onto a lined baking dish and press start. Cook for 12 minutes until lightly browned. Serve.

DIJON HERB SALMON

Cooking Time: 15 minutes

Serves: 4

Ingredients:
- 4 salmon fillets
- 1 tsp dried thyme
- 2 tbsp fresh lemon juice
- 2 tbsp dijon mustard
- 2 tomatoes, sliced
- 1 small onion, sliced
- 1 tsp dried oregano
- 1 tsp dried rosemary
- Pepper
- Salt

Directions:
1. Spray a baking dish with cooking spray and set aside.
2. Insert wire rack in rack position 6. Select bake, set temperature 390 f, timer for 15 minutes. Press start to preheat the oven.
3. In a bowl, mix together lemon juice, oregano, rosemary, thyme, mustard, pepper, and salt.
4. Add fish fillets and coat well form both sides. Cover and place in the refrigerator for 30 minutes.
5. Arrange sliced tomatoes and onion in the baking dish then place marinated fish fillets on top. Pour remaining marinade over fish fillets.
6. Bake for 15 minutes.
7. Serve and enjoy.

MEAT RECIPES

AIR FRYER BEEF CASSEROLE

Cooking Time: 30 minutes

Serves: 4

Ingredients:
- 1 green bell pepper, seeded and chopped
- 1 onion, chopped
- 1-lb. Ground beef
- 3 cloves of garlic, minced
- 3 tbsp. Olive oil
- 6 cups eggs, beaten
- Salt and pepper to taste

Directions:
1. Preheat the smart air fryer oven for 5 minutes at 325°f.
2. In a baking dish, mix the ground beef, onion, garlic, olive oil, and bell pepper
3. Season with salt and pepper and pour in the beaten eggs and give a good stir.
4. Place the dish with the beef and egg mixture in the air fryer.
5. Pour into the oven basket and place the rack on the middle-shelf of the smart air fryer oven.
6. Set temperature to 325°f, and set time to 30 minutes.
7. Bake for 30 minutes.

CHARREd ONIONS & STEAK CUBE BBQ

Cooking Time: 40 minutes

Serves: 3

Ingredients:
- 1 cup red onions cut into wedges
- 1 tbsp. Dry mustard
- 1 tbsp. Olive oil
- 1-lb. Boneless beef sirloin, cut into cubes
- Salt and pepper to taste

Directions:
1. Preheat the air fryer to 390°f.
2. Place the grill rack in the air fryer. Toss all ingredients In a bowl and mix until everything is coated with the seasonings.
3. Place on the grill rack and cook for 40 minutes.
4. Halfway through the cooking time, give a stir to cook evenly.

BEEF RIBEYE STEAK

Cooking Time: 10 minutes

Serves: 4

Ingredients:
- 4 (8-oz.) rib-eye steaks
- 1 tbsp. Mccormick grill mates montreal steak seasoning
- Salt and pepper to taste

Directions:
1. Season the steaks with the seasoning and salt and pepper to taste.
2. Place 2 steaks in the smart air fryer oven grill rack and cook for 5 minutes.
3. Open the air fryer and flip the steaks — cook for an additional 5 minutes.
4. Remove the cooked steaks from the smart air fryer oven, then repeat for the remaining two steaks. Serve warm.

AIR FRYER ROAST BEEF

Cooking Time: 20 minutes

Serves: 6

Ingredients:
Roast beef
1 tbsp. Olive oil
Seasonings of choice

Directions:
1. Preheat your smart air fryer oven to 160 °f.
2. Place the beef roast in a bowl and toss with olive oil and desired seasonings.
3. Put seasoned roast into the air fryer and set the temperature to 160°f, time to 20 minutes.
4. Halfway through cooking, turn the roast when the timer sounds and cook another 10 minutes.

PARMESAN BREAdEd PORK CHOPS

Cooking Time: 12 minutes

Serves: 5

Ingredients:
- 5 (3½- to 5-oz.) pork chops (bone-in)
- 1 tsp. Italian seasoning
- Salt and pepper to taste
- ¼ cup all-purpose flour
- 2 tbsp. Italian bread crumbs
- 3 tbsp. Finely grated parmesan cheese
- Cooking oil

Directions:
1. Preheat the oven at 400 °f
2. Season the pork chops with the italian seasoning and seasoning salt and pepper to taste.
3. Sprinkle the flour on both sides of the pork chops, and then coat both sides with the bread crumbs and parmesan cheese.
4. Place the pork chops in the oven and spray them with cooking oil.
5. Cook for 6 minutes.
6. Open the air fryer oven and flip the pork chops then cook for an additional 6 minutes.
7. Cool before serving.

BREAdEd PORK CHOPS

Cooking Time: 12 minutes

Serves: 8

Ingredients:
- 6 center-cut boneless pork chops
- 1/8 tsp. Pepper
- ¼ tsp. Chilli powder
- ½ tsp. Onion powder
- ½ tsp. Garlic powder
- 1 ¼ tsp. Sweet paprika
- 2 tbsp. Grated parmesan cheese
- 1/3 cups crushed cornflake crumbs
- ½ cups panko breadcrumbs
- 1 beaten egg

Directions:
1. Preheat the oven at 400 °f
2. Spray the basket with olive oil.
3. Season both sides of pork chops with salt, pepper, chili powder, onion powder, garlic powder, paprika, cornflake crumbs, panko breadcrumbs, and parmesan cheese.
4. Beat egg in another bowl.
5. Dip the chops into the egg and then crumb mixture.
6. Add pork chops to air fryer oven and spritz with olive oil.
7. Set time to 12 minutes.
8. Cook, making sure to flip over halfway through the cooking process
9. Enjoy.

ROASTEd PORK TENdERLOIN

Cooking Time: 50 minutes

Serves: 4

Ingredients:
- 3 lb. Pork tenderloin
- 2 tbsp. Extra-virgin olive oil
- 2 garlic cloves, minced
- 1 tsp. Dried basil
- 1 tsp. Dried oregano
- 1 tsp. Dried thyme
- Salt and pepper to taste

Directions:
1. Preheat the oven at 375 °f
2. Drizzle the pork tenderloin with the olive oil.
3. Rub the garlic, basil, oregano, thyme, and salt and pepper to taste all over the tenderloin.
4. Place the tenderloin in the air fryer oven and cook for 40 minutes.
5. Open the air fryer oven and flip the pork tenderloin and cook for an additional 10 minutes.
6. Remove the cooked pork from the air fryer oven and allow it to cool before cutting.

AIR FRYER BEEF BURGERS

Cooking Time: 10 minutes

Serves: 4

Ingredients:
- 1 lb. Lean ground beef
- 1 tsp. Dried parsley
- ½ tsp. Dried oregano
- ½ tsp. Pepper
- ½ tsp. Salt
- ½ tsp. Onion powder
- ½ tsp. Garlic powder
- 1 tsp. Worcestershire sauce

Directions:
1. Preheat the oven at 350 °f
2. Mix all seasonings till combined.
3. Place beef in a bowl and add seasonings then mix well.
4. Make four patties from the mixture and using your thumb, making an indent in the center of each patty.
5. Add patties to the air fryer basket.
6. Set time to 10 minutes, and cook 10 minutes.
7. Enjoy.

BACON-WRAPPEd FILET MIGNON

Cooking Time: 15 minutes

Serves: 2

Ingredients:
- 2 bacon slices
- 2 (4-oz.) filet mignon
- Salt and black pepper, to taste
- Olive oil cooking spray

Directions:
1. Wrap 1 bacon slice around each filet mignon and secure with toothpicks.
2. Season the fillets with the salt and black pepper lightly.
3. Arrange the filet mignon onto a rack and spray with cooking spray.
4. Select "air fry" And then adjust the temperature to 375 °f. Set the timer for 15 minutes and press start.
5. When cooking time is complete, remove the rack from oven and serve hot.

LAMB BURGERS

Cooking Time: 8 minutes

Serves: 6

Ingredients:
- 2 lbs. Ground lamb
- 1 tbsp. Onion powder
- Salt and ground black pepper, to taste

Directions:

1. In a bowl, add all the listed ingredients And mix well.
2. Make six equal-sized patties from the mixture.
3. Arrange the patties onto a cooking tray.
4. Air fry at a temperature of 360 °f. For 8 minutes.
5. When cooking time is complete, remove the tray from the oven and serve hot.

LAMB CHOPS

Cooking Time: 30 minutes
Serves: 4

Ingredients:
- 4 lamb chops
- 1 1/2 tsp tarragon
- 1 1/2 tsp ginger
- 1/4 cup brown sugar
- 1 tsp garlic powder
- 1 tsp ground cinnamon
- Pepper
- Salt

Directions:
1. Insert wire rack in rack position 6. Select bake, set temperature 375 f, timer for 30 minutes. Press start to preheat the oven.
2. Add garlic powder, cinnamon, tarragon, ginger, brown sugar, pepper, and salt into the zip-lock bag and mix well.
3. Add lamb chops in a zip-lock bag. The sealed bag shakes well and places it in the refrigerator for 2 hours.
4. Place marinated lamb chops on a roasting pan and bake for 30 minutes.
5. Serve and enjoy.

MEATBALLS

Cooking Time: 15 minutes

Serves: 4

Ingredients:
- 1 lb ground pork
- 1/2 tsp dried thyme
- 1 tsp paprika
- 1 tsp garlic powder
- 1/2 tsp ground cumin
- 1/2 tsp coriander
- 1 tsp onion powder
- Pepper
- Salt

Directions:
1. Insert wire rack in rack position 6. Select bake, set temperature 390 f, timer for 15 minutes. Press start to preheat the oven.
2. Add all ingredients Into the large bowl and mix until well combined.
3. Make small balls from the meat mixture and place them on a baking tray and bake for 15 minutes.
4. Serve and enjoy.

POULTRY RECIPES

SAUCY GRILLEd CHICKEN

Cooking Time: 25 minutes + marinating time

Serves: 2

Ingredients:
- 2 chicken breasts, cubed
- 1 garlic clove, minced
- ½ cup ketchup
- ½ tbsp fresh ginger, minced
- ½ cup soy sauce
- 2 tbsp sherry
- ½ cup pineapple juice
- 2 tbsp apple cider vinegar
- ½ cup brown sugar

Directions:
1. In a saucepan over low heat, mix ketchup, pineapple juice, sugar, vinegar, soy sauce, sherry, and ginger and stir until heated. Pour the hot sauce over the chicken. Marinate for 15 minutes.
2. Preheat breville on bake function to 360 f. Transfer the chicken in a baking dish and press start. Bake for 15 -20 minutes. Serve warm.

MUSTARd & THYME CHICKEN

Cooking Time: 20 minutes

Serves: 4

Ingredients:
- 1 tsp garlic powder
- 1 lb chicken breasts, sliced
- 1 tsp dried thyme
- ½ cup dry wine
- ½ cup dijon mustard
- 1 cup breadcrumbs
- 1 tbsp lemon zest
- 2 tbsp olive oil

Directions:
1. In a bowl, mix breadcrumbs with garlic powder, lemon zest, salt, and pepper. In another bowl, mix mustard, olive oil, and wine. Dip chicken slices in the wine mixture and then in the crumb mixture. Place the chicken in the basket and cook for 15 minutes at 350 f on airfry function.

AVOCAdO & RAdISH CHICKEN BOWL

Cooking Time: 20 minutes

Serves: 2

Ingredients:
- ½ lb chicken breasts, cubed
- 1 avocado, sliced
- 4 radishes, sliced
- 1 tbsp fresh parsley, chopped
- Salt and black pepper to taste

Directions:
1. Preheat breville on airfry function to 300 degrees f. Combine all ingredients in a baking dish and press start. Cook for 14 minutes. Serve with cooked rice or fried red kidney beans.

WHITE WINE CHICKEN WINGS

Cooking Time: 30 minutes

Serves: 2

Ingredients:
- 8 chicken wings
- ½ tbsp sugar
- 2 tbsp cornflour
- ½ tbsp white wine
- 1 tbsp fresh ginger, grated
- ½ tbsp olive oil

Directions:
1. In a bowl, mix olive oil, ginger, white wine, and sugar. Add in the chicken wings and toss to coat. Roll up in the flour. Place the chicken in the frying basket and press start. Cook for 20 minutes until crispy on the outside at 320 f on airfry function. Serve warm.

GARLIC LEMONY CHICKEN BREAST

Cooking Time: 20 minutes

Serves: 2

Ingredients:
- 1 chicken breast
- 2 lemon, juiced and rind reserved
- 1 tbsp chicken seasoning
- 1 tbsp garlic puree
- A handful of peppercorns
- Salt and black pepper to taste

Directions:
1. Place a silver foil sheet on a flat surface. Add all seasonings alongside the lemon rind. Lay the chicken breast onto a chopping board and trim any fat and little bones; season.
2. Rub the chicken seasoning on both sides. Place on the foil sheet and seal tightly; flatten with a rolling pin. Place the breast in the basket and cook for 15 minutes at 350 f on airfry function.

CRISPY PARMESAN ESCALLOPS

Cooking Time: 20 minutes

Serves: 4

Ingredients:
- 4 skinless chicken breasts
- 1 cup panko breadcrumbs
- ¼ cup parmesan cheese, grated
- 3 fresh sage leaves, chopped
- 1 cup flour
- 2 eggs, beaten

Directions:
1. Place the chicken breasts between 2 sheets of cling film and beat well using a rolling pin to a ¼-inch thickness. In a bowl, mix parmesan cheese, sage, and breadcrumbs.
2. Dip the chicken into the flour and then into the eggs. Finally, dredge into the breadcrumbs mixture. Transfer to the basket and cook in the breville for 14 minutes at 350 f on airfry mode.

SWEET CHINESE CHICKEN WINGETTES

Cooking Time: 25 minutes

Serves: 4

Ingredients:
- 1 lb chicken wingettes
- 1 tbsp fresh cilantro, chopped
- Salt and black pepper to taste
- 1 tbsp roasted peanuts, chopped
- ½ tbsp apple cider vinegar
- 1 garlic clove, minced
- ½ tbsp chili sauce
- 1 ginger, minced
- 1 ½ tbsp soy sauce
- 2 ½ tbsp honey

Directions:
1. Season chicken with salt and black pepper. In a bowl, mix ginger, garlic, chili sauce, honey, soy sauce, cilantro, and vinegar. Cover chicken with honey sauce. Place the prepared chicken in the basket and cook for 20 minutes at 360 f on airfry function. Serve sprinkled with peanuts.

CHICKEN WINGS WITH BUFFALO SAUCE

Cooking Time: 35 minutes

Serves: 4

Ingredients:
- 2 pounds chicken wing
- ½ cup cayenne pepper sauce
- 2 tbsp coconut oil
- 1 tbsp worcestershire sauce
- 1 tbsp kosher salt

Directions:
1. In a bowl, combine cayenne pepper sauce, coconut oil, worcestershire sauce, and salt. Place the chicken in the basket and press start. Cook for 25 minutes at 380 f on air fy function. Increase the temperature to 400 f and cook for 5 more minutes. Transfer into a large-sized bowl and toss in the prepared sauce. Serve with celery sticks and enjoy!

COCONUT CHICKEN BREASTS

Cooking Time: 25 minutes

Serves: 4

Ingredients:
- 4 chicken breasts, cubed
- 1 cup coconut flakes
- 3 eggs, beaten
- ½ cup cornstarch
- Salt and black pepper to taste
- 1 tsp cayenne pepper powder

Directions:
1. In a bowl, mix salt, cornstarch, cayenne and black peppers. In another bowl, combine eggs and coconut flakes. Rub the chicken with pepper mix and dredge it in the egg mix. Place the chicken in the greased basket and press start. Cook for 20 minutes at 350 f on airfry function. Serve.

ASIAN-STYLE CHICKEN dRUMSTICKS

Cooking Time: 25 minutes

Serves: 4

Ingredients:
- 8 chicken drumsticks
- 2 tbsp olive oil
- 1 tbsp sesame oil
- 4 tbsp honey
- 3 tbsp light soy sauce
- 2 garlic cloves, crushed
- 1 small knob fresh ginger, grated
- 1 small bunch cilantro, chopped
- 2 tbsp sesame seeds, toasted

Directions:
1. Add all ingredients in a freezer bag, except for sesame seeds and cilantro. Seal and massage until drumsticks are well coated. Preheat breville to 400 f on airfry function.
2. Place the drumsticks in the basket and press start. Cook for 18-20 minutes. Sprinkle with sesame seeds and cilantro to serve.

CHICKEN WINGS WITH CHILI-LIME SAUCE

Cooking Time: 25 minutes

Serves: 2

Ingredients:
- 10 chicken wings
- 2 tbsp hot chili sauce
- ½ tbsp lime juice
- Salt and black pepper to taste

Directions:
1. Preheat breville on airfry function to 350 f. Mix lime juice and chili sauce. Toss in the chicken wings. Transfer them to the basket and press start. Cook for 25 minutes. Serve.

CHICKEN WINGS WITH HONEY & CASHEW CREAM

Cooking Time: 25 minutes

Serves: 4

Ingredients:
- 2 lb chicken wings
- 1 tbsp fresh cilantro, chopped
- Salt and black pepper to taste
- 1 tbsp cashews cream
- 1 garlic clove, minced
- 1 tbsp plain yogurt
- 2 tbsp honey
- ½ tbsp white wine vinegar
- ½ tbsp ginger, minced
- ½ tbsp garlic chili sauce

Directions:
1. Preheat breville on airfry function to 360 f. Season the wings with salt and black pepper, place them in a baking dish. Press start and cook for 15 minutes. In a bowl, mix the remaining ingredients. Top the chicken with sauce and cook for 5 more minutes. Serve warm.

CHICKEN & CHEESE ENCHILAdA

Cooking Time: 35 minutes

Serves: 4

Ingredients:
- 1 lb chicken breasts, chopped
- 2 cups cheddar cheese, grated
- ½ cup salsa
- 1 can green chilies, chopped
- 12 flour tortillas
- 2 cups enchilada sauce

Directions:
1. In a bowl, mix salsa and enchilada sauce. Toss in the chopped chicken to coat. Place the chicken on the tortillas and roll; top with cheese. Place the prepared tortillas in a baking tray and press start. Cook for 25-30 minutes at 400 f on bake function. Serve with guacamole and hot dips!

BALSAMIC CHICKEN WITH MOZZARELLA CHEESE

Cooking Time: 25 minutes

Serves: 4

Ingredients:
- 4 chicken breasts, cubed
- 4 fresh basil leaves
- ¼ cup balsamic vinegar
- 2 tomatoes, chopped
- 1 tbsp butter, melted
- 4 mozzarella cheese, grated

Directions:
1. In a bowl, mix butter and balsamic vinegar. Add in the chicken and toss to coat. Transfer to a baking tray and press start. Cook for 20 minutes at 400 f on airfry function. Top with mozzarella cheese and bake until the cheese melts. Top with basil and tomatoes and serve.

PARMESAN COATEd CHICKEN CUTLETS

Cooking Time: 30 minutes

Serves: 4

Ingredients:
- ¼ cup parmesan cheese, grated
- 4 chicken cutlets
- ⅛ tbsp paprika
- ¼ tsp pepper
- 2 tbsp panko breadcrumbs
- 1 tbsp parsley
- ½ tbsp garlic powder
- 2 large eggs, beaten

Directions:
1. In a bowl, mix parmesan cheese, breadcrumbs, garlic powder, pepper, and paprika. Add eggs to another bowl. Dip the chicken cutlets in the eggs, dredge them in cheese/panko mixture and place them in the basket. Press start and cook for 20-25 minutes on airfry function at 400 f until crispy.

VEGETABLES

JALAPEÑO POPPERS

Cooking Time: 10 minutes
Serves: 4

Ingredients:
- 16 whole fresh jalapeño
- 1 cup nonfat refried beans
- 1 cup shredded monterey jack
- 1 scallion, sliced
- 1 tsp. Salt, divided
- 1/4 cup all-purpose flour
- 2 large eggs
- 1/2 cup fine cornmeal
- Olive oil cooking spray

Directions:
1. Slice each jalapeño lengthwise on one side.
2. Place the jalapeños side by side in a microwave-safe bowl and microwave them for 5 minutes until they are slightly soft.
3. Mix refried beans, scallions, 1/2 tsp. Salt and cheese in a bowl.
4. Once your jalapeños are softened, you can scoop out the seeds and add one tbsp of your refried bean mixture.
5. Press the jalapeño closed around the filling.
6. Beat your eggs in a small bowl and place your flour in a separate bowl. In a third bowl, mix your cornmeal and the remaining salt.
7. Roll each pepper in the flour, then the egg, and finally in the cornmeal.
8. Place the peppers on a flat surface and coat them with a cooking spray; olive oil cooking spray is suggested.
9. Pour into the oven rack/basket.
10. Place the rack on the middle-shelf of the smart air fryer oven. Set temperature to 400°f, and set time to 5 minutes.
11. Select start/stop to begin.
12. Turn each pepper and then cook for another 5 minutes.
13. Serve hot.

AIR FRIEd CAULIFLOWER RICE

Cooking Time: 20 minutes
Serves: 4

Ingredients:

Round 1:
- 1 tsp. Turmeric
- 1 cup diced carrot
- ½ cup diced onion
- 2 tbsp. Low-sodium soy sauce
- ½ block of extra firm tofu

Round 2:
- ½ cups frozen peas
- 2 minced garlic cloves
- ½ cups chopped broccoli
- 1 tbsp. Minced ginger
- 1 tbsp. Rice vinegar
- 1½ tsp. Sesame oil
- 2 tbsp. Reduced-sodium soy sauce
- 3 cups riced cauliflower

Directions:
1. Preheat the smart air fryer oven to 370 °f
2. Crumble tofu in a large bowl and toss with the entire round one ingredient.
3. Place the baking dish in the smart air fryer oven cooking basket, set the temperature to 370°f, and set time to 10 minutes and cook 10 minutes, making sure to shake once.
4. In another bowl, toss ingredients From round 2 together.
5. Add round 2 mixture to air fryer and cook for another 10 minutes, ensuring to shake 5 minutes in
6. Enjoy!

AIR FRIEd THYME POTATOES

Cooking Time: 20 minutes
Serves: 4

Ingredients:
- 1 lb. Small red potatoes cut into 1-inch pieces
- 1 tbsp. Olive oil
- 2 tsp. Fresh thyme, chopped
- Salt and ground black pepper, to taste
- 1 tbsp. Lemon zest, grated

Directions:
1. In a bowl, add all the listed ingredients Except lemon zest and toss to coat thoroughly.
2. Place the potatoes in the basket.
3. Select air fry and then adjust the temperature to 400°f. Set the timer for 20 minutes and press start.
4. When ready, transfer the potatoes into a bowl.
5. Add the lemon zest and toss to coat thoroughly.
6. Serve immediately.

BUTTEREd CAULIFLOWER

Cooking Time: 15 minutes
Serves: 4

Ingredients:
- 1 lb. Cauliflower head, cut into florets
- 1 tbsp. Butter, melted
- ½ tsp. Red pepper flakes, crushed
- Salt and ground black pepper, to taste

Directions:
1. In a bowl, add all the listed ingredients And toss to coat thoroughly.

2. Place the cauliflower in the basket.
3. Select air fry and then adjust the temperature to 400°f. Set the timer for 15 minutes and press start.
4. When ready, serve immediately.

TANGY BRUSSELS SPROUT

Cooking Time: 20 minutes
Serves: 4

Ingredients:
- 1 lb. Brussels sprouts trimmed and cut into small pieces
- 1 tbsp. Balsamic vinegar
- 1 tbsp. Olive oil
- Salt and ground black pepper, to taste

Directions:
1. In a bowl, add all the listed ingredients And toss to coat thoroughly.
2. Place the brussels sprouts in the basket.
3. Select air fry and then adjust the temperature to 350°f. Set the timer for 20 minutes and press start.
4. When the timer goes off, remove from the oven and serve hot.

SPICEd ZUCCHINI

Cooking Time: 5 minutes
Serves: 1

Ingredients:
- 1 lb. Zucchini, cut into ½-inch thick slices lengthwise
- 1 tbsp. Olive oil
- ½ tsp. Garlic powder
- ½ tsp. Cayenne pepper
- Salt and ground black pepper, to taste

Directions:
1. In a bowl, add all the listed ingredients And toss to coat thoroughly.
2. Arrange the zucchini slices onto a cooking tray.
3. Select air fry and then adjust the temperature to 400°f. Set the timer for 12 minutes and press start.
4. When cooking time is complete, remove the tray from the oven and serve hot.

GREEN BEANS WITH CARROTS

Cooking Time: 10 minutes
Serves: 3

Ingredients:
- ½ lb. Green beans, trimmed
- ½ lb. Carrots, peeled and cut into sticks
- 1 tbsp. Olive oil
- Salt and ground black pepper, to taste

Directions:
1. In a bowl, add all the listed ingredients And toss to coat thoroughly.
2. Place the vegetables in the basket.
3. Air fry at a temperature of 400°f for 10 minutes
4. When ready, serve.

MIXEd VEGGIES COMBO

Cooking Time: 18 minutes
Serves: 4

Ingredients:
- 1 cup baby carrots
- 1 cup broccoli florets
- 1 cup cauliflower florets
- 1 tbsp. Olive oil
- 1 tbsp. Italian seasoning
- Salt and ground black pepper, to taste

Directions:
1. In a bowl, add all the listed ingredients Then toss to coat thoroughly.
2. Place the vegetables in the basket.
3. Place the roasting pan on a lower rack to catch the drips
4. Select air fry and then adjust the temperature to 380°f and time to 18 minutes.
5. When ready, serve immediately.

SAGE HONEY SWEET POTATOES

Cooking Time: 45 minutes
Serves: 8

Ingredients:
- 4 large sweet potatoes, peel and cut into 1-inch cubes
- 2 tbsp olive oil
- 10 sage leaves
- 1 tsp honey
- 2 tsp vinegar
- 1/4 tsp paprika
- 1/2 tsp sea salt

Directions:
1. Insert wire rack in rack position 6. Select bake, set temperature 375 f, timer for 35 minutes. Press start to preheat the oven.
2. Toss sweet potato with olive oil, sage, leaves, and salt in the roasting pan and bake for 35 minutes.
3. Toss sweet potatoes and bake for 10 minutes more.
4. Add honey, vinegar, and paprika and toss well.
5. Serve and enjoy.

GREEK ROASTEd BROCCOLI

Cooking Time: 15 minutes
Serves: 4

Ingredients:
- 4 cups broccoli florets
- 1 tbsp fresh lemon juice
- 1/2 tsp lemon zest
- 2 garlic cloves, minced
- 1 tbsp olive oil
- 2 tsp capers, rinsed
- 1 tsp dried oregano
- 10 olives, pitted and sliced
- 1 cup cherry tomatoes
- 1/4 tsp salt

Directions:
1. Insert wire rack in rack position 6. Select bake, set temperature 390 f, timer for 15 minutes. Press start to preheat the oven.
2. In a bowl, toss broccoli, garlic, oil, tomatoes, and salt.
3. Spread broccoli mixture on roasting pan and bake for 15 minutes.
4. In a large bowl, mix together lemon juice, capers, oregano, olives, and lemon zest. Add roasted broccoli and tomatoes and stir well.
5. Serve and enjoy.

BALSAMIC CAULIFLOWER

Cooking Time: 25 minutes
Serves: 4

Ingredients:
- 8 cups cauliflower florets
- 1 tsp dried marjoram
- 2 tbsp olive oil
- 1/2 cup parmesan cheese, shredded
- 2 tbsp balsamic vinegar
- Pepper
- Salt

Directions:
1. Insert wire rack in rack position 6. Select bake, set temperature 390 f, timer for 20 minutes. Press start to preheat the oven.
2. In a bowl, toss cauliflower, marjoram, oil, pepper, and salt.
3. Spread cauliflower on roasting pan and bake for 20 minutes.
4. Toss cauliflower with cheese and vinegar and bake for 5 minutes more.
5. Serve and enjoy.

SNACKS & APPETIZERS

ONION STRUdEL

Cooking Time: 15 minutes
Serves: 5

Ingredients:
- 12 sheets phyllo dough
- 3 tbsp. Olive oil
- 1 egg
- 1 lb. Mushrooms
- 1 medium onion
- Leaves from 1 sprig of thyme
- 6 tbsp. Freshly grated parmesan
- Salt and pepper to taste
- 3 tbsp. Butter
- 1 tbsp. Dry sherry
- 1 tbsp. All-purpose flour

Directions:
1. Preheat the air fryer oven to 400°f.
2. Line a baking sheet with parchment paper.
3. Pour oil into a skillet on medium heat and sauté mushrooms and onions for about 7 minutes.
4. Add sherry and cook for another 3 minutes.
5. Mix in the flour, thyme salt, and pepper and remove from heat.
6. Melt butter in a small sauté pan. Brush one half of the phyllo sheet lengthwise with butter.
7. Fold the side with butter over the side without and smooth out any wrinkles or bubbles.
8. Again, brush one half of the phyllo with butter, and fold the unbuttered side over it again.
9. Place one spoonful of mushroom filling at the end of the column and sprinkle parmesan on top.
10. Fold a corner over the filling to create a triangle shape and keep folding over triangles (like folding a flag).
11. Beat the egg and brush it over the strudel triangle.
12. Repeat for as many strudels that will fit on a baking sheet and bake for 15 minutes.

PARMESAN BAKEd ONION

Cooking Time: 1 hour 15 minutes
Serves: 6

Ingredients:
- 1 (20-oz.) bag hash browns, shredded
- 3 green onions
- 1/2 cup grated parmesan cheese
- 1 tsp. Kosher salt
- 1/2 tsp. Black pepper
- 2 tbsp. Olive oil

Directions:
1. Chop the green onions.
2. Preheat air fryer oven to 350°f.
3. Combine hash browns, cheese, onion, salt, and pepper in a large bowl.
4. Drizzle olive oil over the hash mixture and toss with a fork.
5. Grease a muffin tin and spoon mixture into the tin.
6. Pack mixture into each cup by pushing it down with the rounded side of the spoon
7. Bake for 1 hour, 15 minutes
8. Serve warm.

GARLIC KALE CHIPS

Cooking Time: 10 minutes
Serves: 2

Ingredients:
- 4 cups kale, torn into 1-inch pieces
- 1 tbsp. Olive oil
- 1/4 tsp. Pepper
- 1/4 tsp. Garlic powder
- Salt to taste

Directions:
1. Preheat the air fryer oven to 350°f.
2. In a bowl
3. add all the listed ingredients, and toss well.
4. Bake for 10 minutes.

PITA CHIPS

Cooking Time: 8 minutes
Serves: 1

Ingredients:
- 1 whole-wheat pita
- 1 tsp. Olive oil
- Salt to taste

Directions:
1. Preheat the air fryer oven to 375°f.
2. Brush both sides of pita with oil and sprinkle with salt.
3. Cut pita into 6 wedges.
4. Place the pita on a baking sheet(ungreased) and bake for 8 minutes.
5. Enjoy.

ALMOND ONION RINGS

Cooking Time: 15 minutes
Serves: 3

Ingredients:
- ½ cup almond flour
- ¾ cup of coconut milk
- 1 large white onion, sliced into rings
- 1 egg, beaten
- 1 tbsp. Baking powder
- 1 tbsp. Smoked paprika
- Salt and pepper to taste

Directions:
1. Preheat the smart air fryer oven for 5 minutes.
2. In a mixing bowl, mix the almond flour, baking powder, smoked paprika, salt, and pepper.
3. In another bowl, combine the eggs and coconut milk.
4. Soak the onion slices into the egg mixture.
5. Dredge the onion slices in the almond flour mixture.
6. Pour into the oven rack/basket.
7. Set temperature to 325°f, and set time to 15 minutes.
8. Select start/stop to begin.
9. Shake the fryer basket for even cooking.

JICAMA FRIES

Cooking Time: 5 minutes
Serves: 8

Ingredients:
- 1 tbsp. Dried thyme
- ¾ cups arrowroot flour
- ½ large jicama
- 2 eggs

Directions:
1. Slice jicama into fries.
2. Whisk eggs together and pour over fries, then toss to coat.
3. Mix the salt, thyme, and arrowroot flour.
4. Toss egg-coated jicama into dry mixture, tossing to coat thoroughly.
5. Spray the air fryer oven basket with olive oil and add fries.
6. Set temperature to 350°f and set time to 5 minutes.
7. Toss halfway into the cooking process.
8. Serve warm

AIR FRIEd CHICKPEAS

Cooking Time: 17 minutes
Serves: 6

Ingredients:
- 1 (15-oz.) can of chickpeas, rinsed, drained and pat dried
- 1 tsp. Olive oil
- 1 tbsp. Dry ranch seasoning mix

Directions:
1. Place the chickpeas onto a cooking tray and spread in an even layer.
2. Select "Air fry" And then adjust the temperature to 390°f. Set the timer for 9 minutes and

press start.
3. Remove the chickpeas and drizzle them with oil and toss to coat thoroughly.
4. Return the cooking tray to the cooking chamber for 8 minutes.
5. When cooking time is complete, remove the tray from the oven and transfer the chickpeas into a bowl.
6. Toss with the ranch seasoning to coat thoroughly.
7. Serve cold.

BANANA CHIPS

Cooking Time: 10 minutes
Serves: 8

Ingredients:
- 2 raw bananas, peeled and sliced
- 2 tbsp. Olive oil
- Salt and black pepper, to taste

Directions:
1. Coat the banana slices with oil evenly.
2. Preheat the oven to 355°f
3. Arrange the banana slices in the basket in a single layer.
4. Select "air fry" And set the temperature to 355°f for 10 minutes.
5. Select start/cancel to begin cooking.
6. When ready, transfer the banana chips onto a platter and sprinkle with salt and black pepper. Serve warm.

BAKEd OKRA

Cooking Time: 15 minutes
Serves: 4

Ingredients:
- 1 lb fresh okra, cut into 3/4-inch pieces
- 1 tsp paprika
- 1/4 tsp chili powder
- 2 tbsp olive oil
- Salt

Directions:
1. Line roasting pan with parchment paper and set aside.
2. Insert wire rack in rack position 6. Select bake, set temperature 390 f, timer for 15 minutes. Press start to preheat the oven.
3. Add okra, chili powder, paprika, oil, and salt into the bowl and toss well.
4. Spread okra on a roasting pan and bake for 15 minutes.
5. Serve and enjoy.

SALMON CROQUETTES

Cooking Time: 7 minutes
Serves: 4

Ingredients:
- 1 lb can red salmon, drained and mashed
- 2 eggs, beaten
- 1/3 cup olive oil
- 1 cup breadcrumbs

Directions: :
1. Insert wire rack in rack position 4. Select air fry, set temperature 400 f, timer for 7 minutes. Press start to preheat the oven.
2. In a bowl, add drained salmon, eggs, and parsley. Mix well.
3. In a shallow dish, combine together breadcrumbs and oil.
4. Make 16 croquettes from the salmon mixture and coat with breadcrumbs.
5. Place coated croquettes in the air fryer basket and air fry for 7 minutes.
6. Serve and enjoy.

CRISPY BROCCOLI FLORETS

Cooking Time: 10 minutes
Serves: 3

Ingredients:
- 1 lb broccoli florets
- 2 tbsp plain yogurt
- 1 tbsp chickpea flour
- 1/2 tsp red chili powder
- 1/4 tsp turmeric powder
- 1/2 tsp salt

Directions:
1. Insert wire rack in rack position 4. Select air fry, set temperature 400 f, timer for 10 minutes. Press start to preheat the oven.
2. Add all ingredients To the bowl and toss well.
3. Place marinated broccoli in a refrigerator for 15 minutes.
4. Place marinated broccoli into the air fryer basket and air fry for 10 minutes.
5. Serve and enjoy.

EGGPLANT FRIES

Cooking Time: 20 minutes
Serves: 4

Ingredients:
- 1 eggplant, cut into 3-inch pieces
- 1 tbsp olive oil
- 4 tbsp cornstarch
- 2 tbsp water
- Salt

Directions:
1. Insert wire rack in rack position 4. Select air fry, set temperature 390 f, timer for 20 minutes. Press start to preheat the oven.
2. In a bowl, mix together water, oil, eggplant, and cornstarch.
3. Place eggplant fries in the air fryer basket and air fry for 20 minutes.
4. Serve and enjoy.

FISH NUGGETS

Preparation time: 10 minutes
Cooking Time: 20 minutes
Serves: 4

Ingredients:
- 1 lb cod fillet, cut into nuggets
- 1 cup almond flour
- 1 cup breadcrumbs
- 4 tbsp olive oil
- 3 eggs, beaten
- 1 tsp salt

Directions:
1. Insert wire rack in rack position 4. Select air fry, set temperature 490 f, timer for 20 minutes. Press start to preheat the oven.
2. Add beaten eggs in a bowl.
3. Add almond flour in a shallow dish.
4. In another bowl, combine together breadcrumbs, salt, and oil.
5. Coat fish pieces with flour then dip in eggs and finally coat with breadcrumbs.
6. Place coated fish nuggets in the air fryer basket and air fry for 20 minutes.
7. Serve and enjoy.

HERB CHICKEN WINGS

Cooking Time: 15 minutes
Serves: 6

Ingredients:
- 4 lb chicken wings
- 1/4 tsp cinnamon
- 1 habanero, chopped
- 6 garlic cloves, minced
- 2 tbsp soy sauce
- 1 tbsp olive oil
- 4 tbsp vinegar
- 1 fresh lime juice
- 1/2 tbsp ginger, minced
- 1 tbsp brown sugar
- 1 tsp thyme, chopped
- 1/2 tsp white pepper
- 1/2 tsp salt

Directions:
1. Insert wire rack in rack position 4. Select air fry, set temperature 390 f, timer for 15 minutes. Press start to preheat the oven.

2. Add all ingredients Into the mixing bowl and mix well.
3. Place marinated chicken wings in a refrigerator for 2 hours.
4. Add chicken wings into the air fryer basket and air fry for 15 minutes.
5. Serve and enjoy.

DESSERTS

APPLE TREAT WITH RAISINS

Cooking Time: 15 minutes

Serves: 4

Ingredients:
- 4 apples, cored
- 1 ½ oz almonds
- ¾ oz raisins
- 2 tbsp sugar

Directions:
1. Preheat breville on bake function to 360 f. In a bowl, mix sugar, almonds, and raisins and blend the mixture using a hand mixer. Fill cored apples with the almond mixture. Place the prepared apples in the basket and press start. Bake for 10 minutes. Serve with powdered sugar.

PAN-FRIEd BANANAS

Cooking Time: 15 minutes

Serves: 6

Ingredients:
- 8 bananas
- 3 tbsp vegetable oil
- 3 tbsp cornflour
- 1 egg white
- ¾ cup breadcrumbs

Directions:
1. Preheat breville on toast function to 350 f. Combine oil and breadcrumbs in a bowl. Coat the bananas with the cornflour, brush with egg white, and dip in the breadcrumb mixture. Arrange on a lined baking sheet and press start. Cook for 8-12 minutes.

DELICIOUS BANANA PASTRY WITH BERRIES

Cooking Time: 15 minutes

Serves: 2

Ingredients:
- 3 bananas, sliced
- 3 tbsp honey
- 2 puff pastry sheets, cut into thin strips
- Fresh berries to serve

Directions:
1. Preheat breville on airfry function to 340 f. Place the banana slices into the cooking basket. Cover with the pastry strips and top with honey. Press start and cook for 10-12 minutes on bake function. Serve with fresh berries.

CINNAMON & HONEY APPLES WITH HAZELNUTS

Cooking Time: 15 minutes

Serves: 2

Ingredients:
- 4 apples
- 1 oz butter
- 2 oz breadcrumbs
- Zest of 1 orange
- 2 tbsp chopped hazelnuts
- 2 oz mixed seeds
- 1 tsp cinnamon
- 2 tbsp honey

Directions:
1. Preheat breville on bake function to 350 f. Core the apples. Make sure to also score their skin to prevent from splitting.
2. Combine the remaining ingredients in a bowl; stuff the apples with the mixture and press start. Bake for 10 minutes. Serve topped with chopped hazelnuts.

MAPLE PECAN PIE

Cooking Time: 1 hr 10 minutes

Serves: 4

Ingredients:
- ¾ cup maple syrup
- 2 eggs
- ½ tsp salt
- ¼ tsp nutmeg
- ½ tsp cinnamon
- 2 tbsp almond butter
- 2 tbsp brown sugar
- ½ cup chopped pecans
- 1 tbsp butter, melted
- 1 8-inch pie dough
- ¾ tsp vanilla extract

Directions:
1. Preheat breville on toast function to 350 f. Coat the pecans with the melted butter. Toast them for 5 minutes. Place the pie crust into the baking pan and scatter the pecans over.
2. Whisk together all remaining ingredients in a bowl. Pour the maple mixture over the pecans. Set breville to 320 f and press start. Bake the pie for 25 minutes on bake function.

EASY MOCHA CAKE

Cooking Time: 30 minutes

Serves: 2

Ingredients:
- ¼ cup butter
- ½ tsp instant coffee
- 1 tbsp black coffee, brewed
- 1 egg

- ¼ cup sugar
- ¼ cup flour
- 1 tsp cocoa powder
- Powdered sugar for icing

Directions:
1. Preheat breville on bake function to 330 f. Beat the sugar and egg together in a bowl. Beat in cocoa, instant and black coffees; stir in flour. Transfer the batter to a greased cake pan and press start. Bake for 15 minutes. Dust with powdered sugar and serve.

APRICOT CRUMBLE WITH BLACKBERRIES

Cooking Time: 30 minutes

Serves: 4

Ingredients:
- 2 ½ cups fresh apricots, de-stoned and cubed
- 1 cup fresh blackberries
- ½ cup sugar
- 2 tbsp lemon juice
- 1 cup flour
- 5 tbsp butter

Directions:
1. Preheat breville on bake function to 360 f. Add the apricot cubes to a bowl and mix with lemon juice, 2 tbsp sugar, and blackberries. Scoop the mixture into a greased dish and spread it evenly.
2. In another bowl, mix flour and remaining sugar. Add 1 tbsp of cold water and butter and keep mixing until you have a crumbly mixture. Pour over the fruit mixture and cook for 20 minutes.

HANdMAdE dONUTS

Cooking Time: 25 minutes

Serves: 4

Ingredients:
- 8 oz self-rising flour
- 1 tsp baking powder
- ½ cup milk
- 2 ½ tbsp butter
- 1 egg
- 2 oz brown sugar

Directions:
1. Preheat breville on bake function to 350 f. In a bowl, beat the butter with sugar until smooth. Whisk in egg and milk. In another bowl, combine the flour with the baking powder.
2. Fold the flour into the butter mixture. Form donut shapes and cut off the center with cookie cutters. Arrange on a lined baking sheet and cook for 15 minutes. Serve with whipped cream.

MOUTHWATERING CHOCOLATE SOUFFLÉ

Cooking Time: 25 minutes

Serves: 2

Ingredients:
- 2 eggs, whites and yolks separated
- ¼ cup butter, melted
- 2 tbsp flour
- 3 tbsp sugar
- 3 oz chocolate, melted

- ½ tsp vanilla extract

Directions:
1. Preheat breville on bake function to 330 f. Beat the yolks along with the sugar and vanilla extract; stir in butter, chocolate, and flour. Whisk the whites until a stiff peak forms.
2. Working in batches, gently combine the egg whites with the chocolate mixture. Divide the batter between two greased ramekins. Press start. Bake for 14-18 minutes.

CHOCO LAVA CAKES

Cooking Time: 20 minutes

Serves: 4

Ingredients:
- 3 ½ oz butter, melted
- 3 ½ tbsp sugar
- 1 ½ tbsp self-rising flour
- 3 ½ oz dark chocolate, melted
- 2 eggs

Directions:
1. Preheat breville on bake function to 375 f. Beat eggs and sugar until frothy. Stir in butter and chocolate; gently fold in the flour.
2. Divide the mixture between 4 buttered ramekins and press start. Bake in the fryer for 10 minutes. Let cool for 2 minutes before turning the cakes upside down onto serving plates.

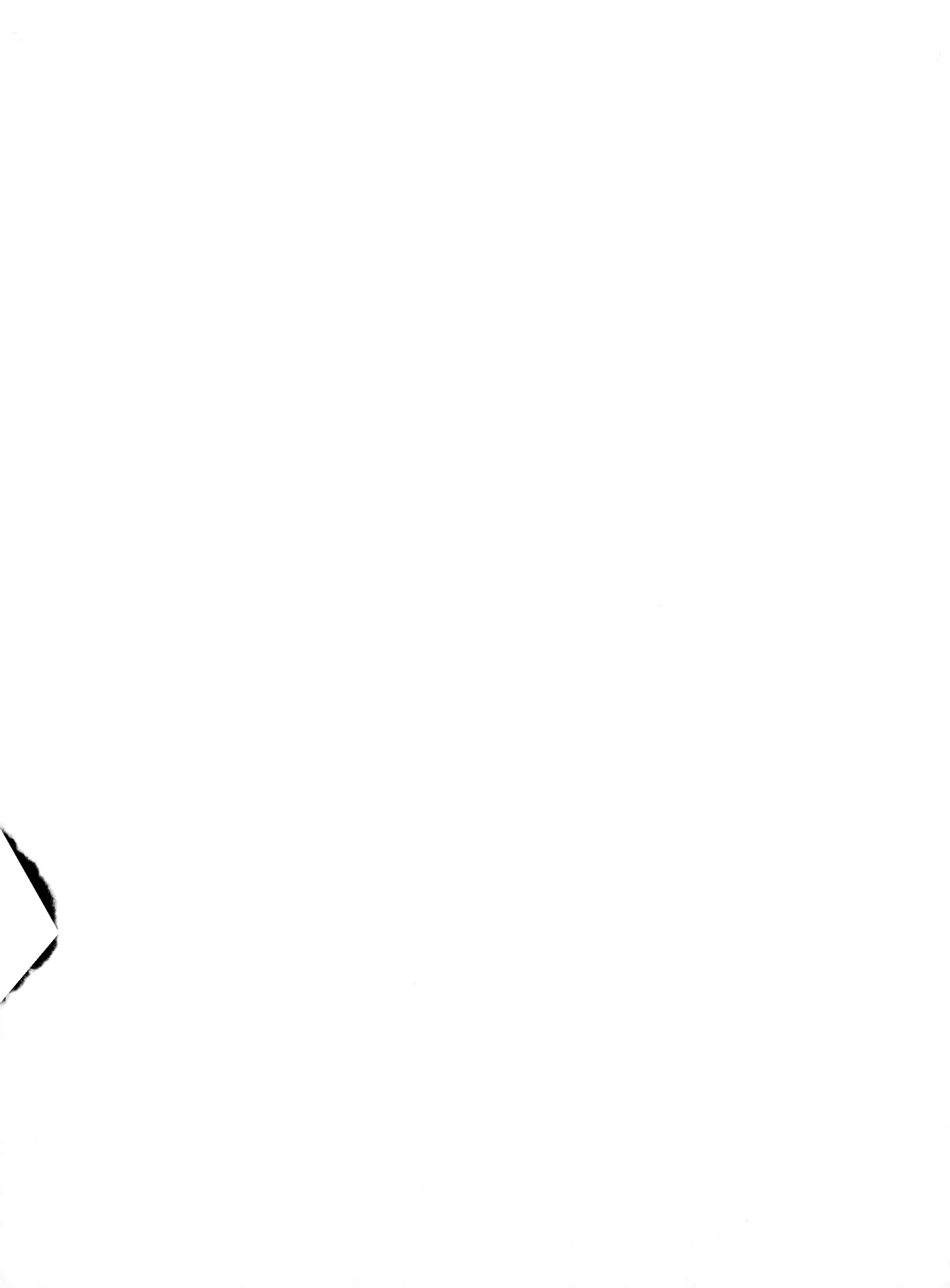

www.ingramcontent.com/pod-product-compliance
Lightning Source LLC
Chambersburg PA
CBHW081120080526
44587CB00021B/3685